THE NEW CAPITALISTS

The New Capitalists

A PROPOSAL TO FREE ECONOMIC

GROWTH FROM THE SLAVERY OF

SAVINGS

by Louis O. Kelso and Mortimer J. Adler

GREENWOOD PRESS, PUBLISHERS
WESTPORT, CONNECTICUT

Library of Congress Cataloging in Publication Data
Kelso, Louis O
  The new capitalists.

    Reprint of the ed. published by Random House, New York.
    1. Capitalism. 2. Finance. 3. United States--
Economic policy. I. Adler, Mortimer Jerome, 1902-
II. Title.
[HB501.K45 1975]   330.12'2   75-14801
ISBN 0-8371-8211-5

Originally published in 1961 by Random House, New York

Reprinted with the permission of Louis O. Kelso

Reprinted in 1975 by Greenwood Press
A division of Congressional Information Service, Inc.
88 Post Road West, Westport, Connecticut 06881

Library of Congress catalog card number 75-14801
ISBN 0-8371-8211-5

Printed in the United States of America

10 9 8 7 6 5 4 3 2

To Betty, Marty, and Katie

CONTENTS

THE NEW CAPITALISTS

1 *Introduction and Definition of Terms*

In *The Capitalist Manifesto,* which we published previously, we outlined a practical program for bringing about the economic changes needed to transform our present mixed economy into a truly capitalist society. Among the measures proposed, one of the most important was the plan for creating new capitalists concurrently with the formation of new capital. This essay, devoted to explaining the financed-capitalist plan, is an attempt to advance our practical thinking about capitalism. It does not add anything except evidence of feasibility to the theory of capitalism as outlined in our earlier book.

Briefly summarized, that theory involves the following propositions: (1) both labor (the human factor) and capital (the non-human factor) are *producers of wealth in the same sense;* (2) the *productiveness* of labor, except for temporary interruptions, has been declining since the dawn of civilization, and the productiveness of capital has been—both relatively and absolutely—increasing, as has the amount of capital employed in production; (3) technological change is the physical process by which the burden of producing wealth is gradually shifted from labor to capital; (4) political and economic freedom in an industrial society depend not merely upon each household's being entitled to *consume* economic goods but upon each household's being entitled to *produce* economic goods; and (5) as labor progressively produces less, and capital progressively produces more, of the gross national product, a growing proportion of all households must participate in production through their ownership of capital and a diminishing number must depend upon the earnings of their labor. (Unemployment, in short, is natural and desirable in technically advanced economies. The task of a capitalist economy is not to fight unemployment at any cost, like a plague. Rather, its objectives should be to make certain that normal technological unemployment falls upon those who can afford it, and to whom it should be the greatest of blessings.)

Two facts must also be kept in mind. The first is that capital produces at least 90 percent of the gross national product in our economy; yet all but a small fraction of the capital instruments are owned (for the most part indirectly through share ownership) by 5 percent of the households of the economy. The second fact is that in spite of this concentration of apparent ownership, 70 percent of the income currently produced is distributed through labor.[1]

These two facts plainly indicate the extent to which private property in capital has been attenuated in its rights. They reveal the extent to which the ownership of capital is being socialized in the American economy. Similar erosion of private property in capital is taking place in all of the industrialized economies of the free world.

It will be our thesis in this essay that our conventional methods of financing corporate enterprises inevitably lead to the socialized ownership of capital. We will try to show that this results from the rigid linkage between the ownership of existing capital and the acquisition of newly formed capital.

The conventional methods of financing new

[1] See *The Capitalist Manifesto*, pp. 257-258.

capital formation involve a systematic concentration of the ownership of productive capital. Since a constantly increasing share of the wealth of the economy is produced by capital, the rights of concentrated ownership arising from conventional finance must be invaded, eroded, and attenuated, if not eventually destroyed; for to give full effect to the rights of such highly concentrated ownership would be to aggregate the great bulk of the annual income of capital in the hands of the capital-owning 5 percent of the households. The ultimate consequence of this would be the disappearance of the mass purchasing power so essential to the maintenance of our mass-production economy. The majority of our population would be plunged into poverty. This, were it to happen, would verify Marx's prediction that capitalism, sowing the seeds of its own destruction, will eventually destroy itself.

The socialization of capital which has gone on apace in the last thirty years has one thing to its credit: it has staved off the immediate failure of our economy as a result of the concentrated ownership of capital. But we do not believe that, in order to save our economy, it is necessary to socialize the ownership of capital. In our opinion, unprecedented economic growth and the restoration of full integrity to private property can be simultaneously brought about by minor changes in our business-financing techniques—changes that will cause them to create a capitalist, instead of a socialist, pattern of ownership. Corporate finance can be made simultaneously to create growth in the number of private owners of capital and growth in newly formed capital. The only limits to growth in either respect would be our manpower (a limitation that is more theoretical than factual), our resources, know-how, and our desire for wealth.

We believe that the existence of a free society in an industrial age depends upon the adoption of the proposed changes in our techniques of financing capital formation. In the course of the following essay, we will deal with other implications of our proposals and with their far-reaching significance.

We will confine ourselves in this essay to fundamental principles that can be simply stated and that have broad application in the field of financing new capital formation. We will try to avoid the use of narrow and specialized terms. Nevertheless, the following simple definitions may be helpful.

A. WEALTH

Wealth consists of anything that is treated as wealth in a society, *i.e.,* anything that is offered for sale or exchange, and for which a demand on the part of potential buyers exists. It includes both goods and services.

There are two radically different kinds of wealth. One, which we may call consumer goods, consists of things or services held or intended for the satisfaction of human wants by the consumer of such goods or services. The period over which consumer goods may render satisfaction can, of course, vary substantially. Food or a service may be wholly consumed at the time of its use, whereas a house or a table may render service to the consumer for decades.

The other basic kind of wealth is capital. Capital items are things held or intended to be used not for immediate satisfaction of human wants, but to produce other goods or services. Capital wealth includes everything used to produce wealth except labor; it is *the non-human factor of production.* The varieties of capital are great indeed, and include such unlike things as land, stores, factories, residential buildings held for rental, tools, machines, railroads, airplanes, ships, mines, etc.

It is both common and practical to include money and credit within the definition of capital, although in the physical sense, neither is productive. The reason for this is that money and credit, being part of our medium of exchange and *repre-*

sentative of wealth, can be speedily converted into productive capital wealth.[2] Furthermore, business practice makes a certain amount of working capital—money or credit—as necessary in the actual production (including distribution) of wealth as any of the forms of productive capital.

B. SAVINGS

The term "savings" is used both in a financial and in a physical sense, but more commonly in the financial sense. It means, in the financial sense, money or credit diverted from immediate use for consumption. Although from the standpoint of the individual saver, savings may be held in the form of money or credit and not used to purchase capital goods, such "sterilization" of savings is and must necessarily be relatively rare. Rather, personal savings are normally invested in capital goods or in a bank, pension fund, insurance company or other financial intermediary which, in turn, perhaps through other financial intermediaries, "invests" or uses the purchasing power thus represented to buy an interest in wealth-producing capital goods.

In the physical sense, "saving" is simply the

[2] Aside from the factor of risk, this is, of course, the basis for the charging and payment of interest.

use of goods or services to produce capital goods rather than for immediate consumption.

Personal savings are savings by individuals. Business or corporate savings are made up of the wealth produced by business or corporate capital that is retained as working capital, or is applied to the acquisition of further capital goods—in the graphic term of the financial world, "new capital formation."

C. INVESTMENT

The act of using money or credit to acquire, either directly or indirectly, an interest in productive capital is called investment.

D. CAPITALISTS

This is a working definition. Its reasonableness and practical significance are fully apparent when one begins to understand the implications of the theory of capitalism. A capitalist is a member of a household which derives not less than half the amount the household spends on consumption from the ownership of capital, *i.e.,* from interest, dividends, rents, royalties, and the like. Not over 1 percent of the households in the American economy would be capitalist households under this definition.[3]

[3] Joseph Livingston, in his book *The American Stock-holder* (1958), p. 35, estimated that about 650,000 households in the economy derive half their income from capital sources.

2 *Traditional System of Financing*
New Capital Formation

That the acquisition of privately owned capital in the United States and throughout the Western world has been financed almost entirely through savings is too well known to deserve documentation. From the early days of industrialization, when these savings were predominantly by individuals, slow changes have taken place in financing techniques in the direction of substituting corporate savings for personal savings in the capital-forming process. The rise of the corporation, the introduction of the personal and corporate income

tax systems and the consequent growing importance of depreciation, depletion, and amortization
procedures have had their influence in bringing
about this shift. So has the growing severity of personal income tax rates, causing corporate shareholders to seek the benefits of accumulation
through indirect capital gain (in the market value
of stock or other assets) which is taxed at a lower
rate, or in some countries not taxed at all. In the
United States, the Federal corporate income tax,
which is imposed solely on the earnings due stockholders, has more than cut in half this potential
source of personal savings of stockholders.

Perhaps of even greater significance in the
trend toward the use of business savings rather
than personal savings to finance new capital formation is the almost universal custom of corporation laws of the Western world to give management discretion to use corporate earnings to finance
expansion rather than pay them out in dividends
to shareholders. So long as personal savings,
brought into the corporate system through the
sale of newly issued common or preferred stocks,
were an important source of funds for capital
formation, the necessity of a satisfactory yield to
shareholders to encourage them to make further
investments acted as a restraining influence on
management's tendency to withhold earnings from
shareholders. However, the sale of newly issued

corporate stock has all but ceased to be an important source of capital funds. Over the ten-year period, 1948-1957, the average annual capital formation by corporations in the United States was 31 billion dollars. Of this, the sale of equity securities for cash averaged 6.2 percent. Common stocks alone accounted on the average during the ten-year period for only 4.6 percent of the total sources of corporate funds.

Yet, it is clear that even this volume would be smaller today if it were not for the stocks of regulated public utility companies which are required by law to use a high proportion of equity financing.

In the year 1958, the sale of corporate stock accounted for 2 billion dollars or 7.2 percent of new capital formation, while 27.5 billion dollars of new capital formation came from internal corporate sources.[4] In the year 1959, the sale of common and preferred stocks together accounted for only 2.5 billion dollars out of aggregate new capital formation by corporations of 47 billion dollars, or 5.3 percent of corporate capital formation. During that year, internal corporate sources, consisting of withheld earnings, depletion allowances, depreciation allowances and amortization allowances, accounted for 30.5 billion dollars

[4] First National City Bank *Newsletter,* August 1959, pp. 91-92.

of the total, and *future* corporate earnings, necessarily obligated to repay some 13.5 billion dollars in debt incurred to finance new capital formation, provided the remaining sources of corporate funds.[5] In general today, about three-fourths of new capital formation is internally generated by corporations, and most of the remainder consists of borrowing against future internally generated funds.

While corporations account for the dominant portion of the production of wealth in the United States, 219.8 billion dollars out of a total of 402.8 billion dollars in 1959,[6] the dependence of new capital formation upon savings is quite the same for unincorporated businesses. Here, however, the savings are still personal, since individuals directly own such businesses.[7]

The change in the United States over the past forty years from the almost exclusive use of personal savings to finance capital formation to the predominant use of corporate funds for this pur-

[5] Economic Report of the President, January 1960, pp. 224, 226.

[6] U. S. Department of Commerce, Office of Business Economics, *Survey of Current Business,* National Income Number, July 1960, p. 14, Table 12. The figures quoted are annual rates for the fourth quarter, seasonally adjusted.

[7] Associations *taxed* as corporations are a technical but unimportant exception.

pose has its own separate significance quite apart from the fact that, *from the standpoint of individuals,* savings still remain the source of capital formation in our economic system. Disregarding the effect upon the concentration of nominal ownership of capital, all funds of corporations, whether withheld earnings, depreciation, depletion, or amortization allowances, are, *from the standpoint of individual members* of the economy, savings; they are funds invested in instruments of production rather than in goods used for consumption by individuals. Because the corporation is legally regarded as an entity, it is treated as the immediate (though not the ultimate) owner of such savings. But in the end, it is the impact upon the individual members of the economy that is important.

The mechanics of finance, both corporate and non-corporate, which connect the formation of capital to savings are familiar to all of us. The individual uses part of his income to buy corporate stocks, or bonds, or notes, and the corporation, using the funds thus acquired, purchases land, plant, equipment, or employs the funds as working capital. The individual proprietors or partners in small businesses use part of their income to invest in capital goods, or mortgage or pledge assets accumulated through previous savings to provide such funds. Corporations and non-corporate businesses, using their allowances against income taxation, and corporations, using earnings withheld from stockholders, purchase capital assets, etc.

The most spectacular uses of existing capital assets (themselves a product of the use of financial savings to effect capital formation) to bring about new capital formation are to be found in the long-term loans made to corporations. These may be secured by liens upon assets or may be made on the strength of the ownership and wealth-producing power of such assets even though the assets themselves are not technically mortgaged or pledged to secure the loan. These loans may or may not be represented by securities, such as corporate bonds, notes or debentures, and they may be made either by great numbers of individuals who purchase corporate debt securities, or by one or more financial intermediaries such as commercial banks, pension trusts, or insurance companies.

In the latter instances, each of the financial intermediaries (*except commercial banks*) will have served as a collector of the financial savings of individuals for the purpose of investment in capital formation. Our commercial banks, however, do not merely invest a portion of savings and deposits of individuals and businesses in new capital formation, subject to the retention of necessary reserves. Through the system of central reserve banking, each dollar of time deposit funds and of bank capital funds may support several dollars—on the average about six dollars—of commercial loans. In this instance, pure credit is employed to finance new capital formation.[8]

To the extent that the credit exceeds the reserve required against the loan, and the loan is not secured by a lien on the corporation's assets, capital formation taking place through a bank term loan is not solely dependent upon current or past savings. Perhaps it would be more accurate to say that in the case of such commercial bank loans new capital formation is to a minor extent (i.e., to the extent of the bank's reserve required to be held against such loans) dependent upon, but not limited to, savings. Such loans, however, will be repaid out of future corporate earnings or other internally generated funds, amounting to an involuntary commitment by stockholders of *future savings*. These involuntary future savings by stockholders take place as the wealth produced by the corporation is applied to repayment of the principal and interest on the bank loan.

[8] Harold G. Moulton in 1935 pointed out that increased capital formation could come about in spite of a decline in savings through the use of commercial bank credit. See *The Formation of Capital*, p. 107.

3 *Function of Savings in the Financing of Capital Formation*

Capital goods are not intended immediately to satisfy any consumer need or desire. They are a form of wealth intended to be used ultimately to *produce* wealth that can be enjoyed by humans— consumer goods and services. It is quite clear, therefore, that the production of capital goods would detract from, rather than contribute to, the purpose for which they were intended unless the wealth which capital produces is in fact a *net* contribution to the output of humanly consumable wealth.

If in a particular enterprise, for example, more wealth is used in producing the capital goods than these goods in turn produce in the form of consumer goods, the net effect of each instance of such capital formation would be to decrease the total output of consumable wealth. Thus, capital formation fails in its purpose unless the wealth produced by the newly formed capital fully equals the cost of the capital goods involved, *and in addition* provides an attractive surplus of wealth beyond. It is the net wealth to be produced by capital that is the motive behind the formation of new capital goods.

From the very nature of capital goods, therefore, it is clear that they would not come into being unless it were expected that through their employment more consumable wealth would be produced than would be laid out in creating the capital goods themselves. *The intent of those who organize the formation of capital is always that the cost of capital goods shall be defrayed from the wealth to be produced by the newly formed capital goods themselves.* Where this expectation is not fulfilled, it is due to the miscalculation of the future by the entrepreneurs—*entrepreneurial error.* Such error may be caused by miscalculation of the forces of supply or demand, failure to estimate competition, engineering errors, incompetent management, unexpected technological change, etc. Among those experienced in business affairs or in rendering advice to entrepreneurs, every precaution is taken to minimize entrepreneurial error.

Let us now consider what useful purpose is served by savings—previously accumulated capital —in this process of new capital formation. Perhaps an example will throw some light on the matter. Suppose we take the case of promoters or entrepreneurs who believe that they can produce an interesting amount of wealth through the establishment of a lumber mill in a particular location. We say that they expect to make a "profit," but it is clear that the essence of their expectation is that the wealth to be created through the new mill will not only "pay off" those who take part in constructing it, and reimburse the costs of labor and supplies and raw materials required to operate it, but will yield an attractive excess that will be shared by the owners of the new mill.

Various things are required to bring about the existence of the new mill. Land must be acquired, machinery and equipment must be purchased or built, the operating and administrative staffs of the business must be employed, sources of timber must be acquired or contracted for, transportation facilities acquired or hired, etc. Of the many different persons whose direct contributions must be induced to bring about the construction of an operating mill, each will fall into one of two classes. Either he is one who expects to be immediately compensated for his contribution (as in the case of workmen who participate in the building of the mill, or suppliers who merely sell materials, supplies or equipment) or he is an investor, *i.e.,* a contributor of something to the project who expects in return an ownership interest. The great majority of those who have anything to do with the enterprise will be men whose current contribution, whether in the form of labor or goods or supplies, must be currently compensated. They either cannot, or are not invited, or do not wish, to become owners of the mill, and their contribution is for immediate compensation.

But who compensates them? The mill is not yet a going concern; it is not yet producing wealth, and even when its production commences, it may be required to operate for years before it will have produced an excess of wealth (a net profit) sufficient to fully defray its costs of formation. The answer, of course, is that the investors shoulder this task. The investors' capital accumulations or savings are put at risk in one way or another to compensate those who take part in bringing about new capital formation and who do so for an immediate payment. We have already touched upon the mechanics of finance through which this comes about. One result is that savings—previous income invested directly or indirectly in capital goods—are used as a source of payment to all who must be compensated for their participation in new capital formation prior to the time when newly formed capital begins to produce wealth in sufficient quantities to reverse the flow of funds. Another result is that those who put their capital or savings at risk generally become the *owners* of the newly formed capital.

So far we have dealt only with the familiar aspects of the function of savings in the financing of capital formation. But a perplexing question now presents itself.

We have seen that capital instruments of whatever nature are designed and intended to produce wealth. They will not come into being unless those who are responsible are satisfied that they will produce wealth equivalent to their cost of production (the aggregate of the market value of the newly formed capital), and a surplus of wealth beyond. This surplus, the net wealth to be produced by capital, is indeed the real reason behind the process of new capital formation.

Why, in our conventional methods of financing new capital formation, is it necessary to depend upon the risking of existing capital (savings) in order to bring into existence newly formed capital that will, in the great majority of instances, produce far more wealth than sufficient to defray its costs of formation? Why is it not adequate to so design the legal structures of our businesses that the wealth produced by newly formed capital instruments will first be applied to reimburse those who have participated in their formation, or, what is the same thing, to reimburse banks which have extended credit for this purpose? Such an arrangement would subordinate the rights of the owners of newly formed capital to the claims of those who have assisted them in bringing such capital instruments into existence, yet would protect the new owners in their receipt of the net wealth to be produced by their newly formed capital.

The answer to this question, of course, is that our conventional methods of financing new capital formation, which involves compensating workers and suppliers who produce the capital instruments from the savings of the prospective new owners, *eliminate entirely* for these workers and suppliers all risk of entrepreneurial error and insure their receipt of compensation for their contributions toward such construction. Or, what is the same thing, banks or other immediate advancers of funds to workmen, suppliers, etc., are insured against loss by existing capital furnished as "security" in one form or another.

In fact, many of our forms of corporate finance involve what might be termed *double insurance*. For example, where the owners of savings invest in the common stock of a corporation, and the corporation employs a contractor to build a mill, both the newly invested savings, which become assets of the corporation for which its stock is issued, as well as the wealth to be produced by the newly constructed mill, are subject to the claims of the contractor for payment for the mill. The same is true if a corporation with assets or earning power sufficient to convince lenders that it can repay debt borrows funds to build a new mill. Both its existing assets (savings made by the business from the standpoint of the corporation's stockholders), and its newly acquired assets, as well as wealth thereafter produced by its increased capital assets, are subject to the legal claims of the contractor for compensation.

Today, therefore, our techniques of financing capital formation are such that two things are insisted upon:

(1) *Convincing evidence that the newly formed capital will produce sufficient wealth, in addition to its own costs of production, to warrant going forward with the project.* This is true whether the new capital to be brought into existence involves the expansion of an existing business or the creation of a new one. This we may call evidence of economic feasibility, evidence that the newly formed capital will produce not only sufficient wealth to reimburse those who have participated

in its production, but also to satisfy reasonable expectations of an excess beyond—a net output of wealth.

(2) *A committing of existing savings or capital toward the reimbursement of the workers, materialmen, vendors of land, suppliers of machinery and equipment, suppliers of legal and accounting services, and others who participate in the formation of new capital.* Thus, these persons who are currently, or almost currently, compensated for their contributions toward new capital formation are insured against the risk of entrepreneurial error, or risk of error in determining economic feasibility. The physical process of new capital formation is one requiring the co-operation of many persons in addition to those who anticipate becoming the owners of the newly formed capital. The functional use of the savings or capital of the prospective new owners is to insure the immediate compensation of these co-operators and protect them from the risk of entrepreneurial error.

Apparently the close connection, regarded as necessary under accepted financing methods, between savings or existing wealth and new capital formation exists for the reason that resort to such savings is the *only* method devised or generally acceptable today for insuring against the risk of entrepreneurial error in the process of new capital formation.

New capital formation requires either that the workers, suppliers of materials, owners of land, suppliers of professional services, and others whose economic contributions are necessary, shall await their reimbursement until the newly formed capital produces sufficient wealth to pay them, or that others shall do the waiting and assume the risk of entrepreneurial error. Since these "co-operators" whose services or goods are needed to produce the newly formed capital are ordinarily unable or unwilling to defer receipt of payment for their contributions toward production and to assume the risk of possible non-payment through entre- preneurial error of the promotors or managers of the firm, the owners of existing capital or savings become the advancers of funds and the insurers in this situation. In the course of so doing, and as a reward for so doing, they become the owners of the newly formed capital.

4 *Consequences of the Traditional Financing Methods*

A. CONCENTRATION OF OWNERSHIP OF CAPITAL

The most obvious, and certainly the most distressing, consequence of a system which rigidly links the formation and ownership of new capital to the ownership of existing capital is the progressive concentration of the ownership of capital. Once we state the proposition that the ownership of savings (capital) is a condition precedent to becoming the owner of newly formed capital and that the magnitude of one is directly proportionate to that of the other, then it follows that increasing industrialization is synonymous with growing concentration of the ownership of capital. It is this relationship between the ownership of existing capital and the ownership of newly formed capital which explains why, in spite of the ownership of some capital by perhaps 15 percent of the households of the economy, the great bulk of capital is owned by 3 or 4 percent of the households.

Since the ownership of capital can be concentrated to any degree, while the ownership of labor cannot be concentrated at all except in a slave society, the problem of the concentration of the ownership of capital would exist under our conventional financing techniques *without regard to any change in the productiveness of capital.* We can only speculate as to how much more severe is this tendency toward concentration where relentless progressive technological change increases the productivity of capital in relation to the declining productivity of labor. The present ownership of productive capital becomes the basis for the future ownership of even more productive capital, and the process is repeated over and over again.

The tendency is quite the same whether the savings of individuals are used to acquire the ownership of newly formed capital, or whether the assets of a corporation are used in financing expansion in such manner that the existing pattern of stock ownership is unchanged and existing stockholders become the ultimate owners of the newly formed capital.

Nor does it seem likely that the spiraling concentration of ownership of capital can be seriously impeded by the meager efforts on the part of the household of modest means to withhold some funds from consumption and accumulate savings. The small saver has open to him in today's economy investment opportunities that are more apt to concentrate the ownership of capital by others than to make him an owner of capital. He may deposit his savings in a savings bank, or he may buy one of the widely advertised types of insurance policy that contains savings or accumulative features, or his employer may invest a portion of his income for him in a pension fund that in turn may be used to purchase interests in capital of one sort or another. In the case of the savings account or the insurance policy, the funds will find their way into new capital formation, but the small saver will receive only a small fixed return that will rarely be more than the erosion resulting from the inflation that is inherent in our full-employment policy. The funds will probably be invested by the bank or the insurance company at market rates of interest in loans to a corporation that derives two or three times that return, or more, on its invested capital.

Every such attempt at saving by the household that is not already the owner of a substantial capital holding contracts consumption. Attempts at saving by the masses drive business and government to devise further consumer credit schemes to raise present spending to support our mass-production industries. Any attempt to make the average household a more effective accumulator of savings in order to enable it to become an owner of productive capital would bring on a recession that would end only when such saving ceased and when large doses of compensatory purchasing power had been artificially injected into the economy.

If one must be an owner of capital to become the owner of newly formed capital, and if the more capital one owns today, the more newly formed capital one can and probably will own tomorrow, then conventional finance is designed to accomplish precisely the opposite of the capitalist dream —a constantly growing number and proportion of households owning viable capital estates. As the burden of production is shifted through technological change from labor to capital, the amount of wealth produced by an almost stationary class of capital owners will continuously increase. In consequence, the maintenance of prosperity and a widely diffused standard of economic well-being will depend upon ever more intensive efforts by government and government-supported power blocs to divert the wealth produced by capital to those who do not own capital. This is the essence of the policy of full employment, and it is the essence of the relentless socialization of the ownership of capital through the *normal* workings of our corporate-financing and business-financing practices.

In *The Capitalist Manifesto,* we called attention to the distinction between the technical efficiency of large-scale production and mere financial efficiency, or market dominance, which on the one hand suppresses competition and may even restrain technological advance, while on the other hand it intensifies the concentration of ownership of capital.[9] Here, in analyzing the relationship between the present ownership of capital and the acquisition of newly formed capital, we are face to face with the mechanics of competition-destroying financial efficiency on the part of corporations.

Consider the following news items selected from among hundreds of similar ones that appear each year:

Capital spending will be stepped up by various companies. Union Carbide said it expects 1960

[9] See *The Capitalist Manifesto,* pp. 213-214.

construction expenditures to "increase appreciably" over the $136 million spent last year. E. J. Thomas, chairman, reported Goodyear Tire & Rubber Co. has authorized capital outlays of $90 million for 1960, compared with expenditures of $55 million out of $78 million authorized for 1959.

Wall Street Journal, February 23, 1960

General Dynamics Corp. and Philadelphia & Reading Corp. agreed "in principle" to set up a jointly-owned company that would produce hydrogen, ammonia, acetylene and other industrial gases and chemicals from Philadelphia & Reading's stocks of anthracite coal waste.

The new company . . . will spend $100 million in plant construction and other capital expenditures . . . "details of the financing of the proposed organization are not yet worked out" but . . . the venture will not require any new financing for Philadelphia & Reading itself . . . each of the parent companies will contribute equity capital to Dynamics Reading, and the joint venture thereafter will do its own financing "through sale of debt and possibly other senior securities." . . .

Wall Street Journal, May 12, 1959

WANTED: $30 MILLION COMPANY

Houston, Texas, April 14. (AP) Reed Roller Bit Co. is shopping around to buy a company with assets up to $30 million.

John Maher, president, said today Reed is hunting an industrial concern and it doesn't necessarily have to be allied with the petroleum industry.

Maher said Reed, an oil tool manufacturing concern, is ready for further diversification.

San Francisco Chronicle, April 15, 1960

William W. Prince, president, disclosed Armour & Co. will undertake large scale expansion, which "will definitely" involve the company's chemical business. He said "We have some $30 million invested in commercial paper and it is not the intention of Armour & Co. to become a bank."

Wall Street Journal, February 23, 1960

The following news item is extracted from an article in *Time* about a very enlightened philanthropist named Charles Dana. Buried in the story is evidence of what our foregoing analysis would lead us to assume.

Why Wait to Die? Dana gets as much fun out of giving as he did out of getting. He was to both manners born, in New York City's fashionable Gramercy Park area of the 1880's. His wealthy banker father financed Pacific whaling fleets, invested in coal mines; his cousin was the *New York Sun*'s famed editor-owner . . . At 36 he reorganized New Jersey's Spicer Manufacturing Co., maker of the first successful universal joint for autos. By the time Spicer was renamed Dana Corp. in 1946, it was a Toledo-based complex of five thriving auto-parts companies. Net sales last year: $168.5 million.

"I found myself with all this money," recalls Board Chairman Dana. "If you wait until you're dead, it often doesn't get used the way you want it to. . . . Why should I let Washington waste it?"   *Time*, December 21, 1959

The following appeared in an article entitled "Khrushchev's Favorite Capitalist." It is about a visit by Russia's Deputy Premier Anastas Mikoyan to Mr. Cyrus Stephen Eaton.

> Now in his twilight years, Cyrus Eaton is the archetype of the fading dog-eat-dog capitalist . . . His personal wealth is estimated at something like $100 million, and his hard-knuckled grip on U.S. industry extends over a $2 billion empire of iron and steel, railroads, shipping, coal and paint.
>   *Time*, January 19, 1959

The following item was contained in an obituary notice on John D. Rockefeller, Jr., who, as the son of a man who gave away 531 million dollars during his life, himself is reported to have given away 478 million dollars to numerous institutions, projects and charities during his lifetime. At his death, taking advantage of the Federal Estate Tax marital deduction, he divided the bulk of his 150-

million-dollar estate equally between his widow and the Rockefeller Brothers Fund, Inc., a charitable foundation:

> Early in life he decided that his mission was to give his vast fortune back to the world, wisely and where it would do the most good. His motivation was not so much simple charity as a religious awareness that wealth is only a trust, and in redistributing the family's gain, he was in a sense carrying out the will of God. At 36, he resigned from half a dozen directorships, and for the next half-century he dedicated his life to philanthropy.
>
> *Time,* May 23, 1960

The next one is extracted from *Fortune:*

MONOPOLKAPITALISMUS?

At the war's end, Allied officials set out to fragment German industry so completely that all the king's horses and all the king's men, let alone Farben and Krupp, couldn't put it back together again. But in October, at a meeting in Cologne of some 800 bankers, businessmen, and government officials, Chancellor Konrad Adenauer stated: "There is great future danger, say in ten or twenty years, of a handful of economic structures controlling the German economy to such a degree that [the government] will be forced to take drastic steps against them."

The Adenauer threat was prompted by a government investigation which indicated that Germany now has only a few big companies that are not dominated by a few big stockholders. Among companies surveyed—1,636 of the country's 2,580 stock firms—34 per cent of their stock was controlled by another company, 45 percent held by "large" stockholders, banks, or the government— leaving but 20 per cent for small investors.

Fortune, December 1958

Each of the foregoing news items, and hundreds of others like them, are mute testimony to a system of financing new capital formation which systematically unifies the present ownership of capital with the ownership of newly formed capital. The particular capital owners who were involved and their advisers can no more be credited with the wisdom of the Almighty in financial matters than they can be charged with a deliberate attempt to destroy the private property base of the economy under which they live. Yet every major increase in new capital formation that is not accompanied by an increase in the number of *new* capitalists is a leap in the direction of socialism!

The great corporations of America think nothing of adding 50 or 100 million dollars to their productive capital in a manner that will not create a single new capital-owning household. The men who accumulate, through this financing system that almost makes it impossible for them not to

accumulate, may with some urging from confisca-
tory gift and estate tax laws, see it as their mission
to give their great fortunes back to the world
where they think it will do the most good. But it
would seem that where the whole progress of
technology is to make capital the predominantly
productive factor in our economy, and to make
ever greater quantities of labor economically
worthless, either it is not important that all men
continue to be economically productive, or the wisdom of the Western world's system of corporation finance is open to question. For clearly it is
concentrating the ownership of the most productive
factor of production in a very few hands, and ever
larger segments of the population must live through
redistribution and charity, however much these are
disguised.

No one is surprised today when the owners of
a hotel suddenly become the owners of a chain of
hotels, nor when the owners of a restaurant become
the owners of a chain of restaurants, nor when the
owners of a warehouse become the owners of a
system of warehouses, nor when the owners of a
supermarket become the owners of a nation-wide
chain of supermarkets, nor when an automobile
company grows to such titanic size that it produces
50 percent of the motor vehicles consumed by the
nation, etc. This is the natural working of a
method of financing new capital formation which

gives newly formed capital almost exclusively to those who already own substantial quantities of it.

Capital is a factor of production in an industrial society. We have estimated that it accounts in America today for the production of not less than 90 percent of the total of all wealth produced.[10] Its productiveness is constantly increasing. By comparison, the productiveness of labor is constantly decreasing, although we use ingenious means through our "full employment" policy to conceal these facts. Capital can serve its function of helping all households to participate in production to a reasonable degree if it is privately owned, if its ownership is widely diffused, and if the number and proportion of households owning viable capital estates grows apace with technological advance. Clearly, our conventional methods of financing new capital formation are ill designed to serve these ends.

B. DENIAL OF ACCESS TO CAPITAL

A free society does not owe every man a living. It may, and undoubtedly should, as a matter of charity, make modest provision for those who cannot produce the wealth they reasonably need to consume. *But its first economic duty to its citizens*

[10] See *The Capitalist Manifesto*, pp. 40-43, 256-265.

is to enable them to be or to become productive.
One does not make men productive by locking
them, through coercive bargaining, into feather-
bedding positions in industry. They are indeed
given the power to become consumers by this
means, but to say that workers are productive
when their labor, in a freely competitive market,
would be worthless, or worth less than enough to
support them, is simply a demoralizing fraud.
Nor are men made productive while they are engaged in any kind of contrived work, whether it is
work creating politically embarrassing surpluses or
work creating war material that better serves the
ends of full employment than the ends of necessary
defense. In fact, one makes men productive
not by granting them wages or a salary, but only
by enabling them to exercise the power to
produce in such manner as to produce goods for
which there is an economic demand. In an industrial society, in which the burden of production
is progressively passing from labor to capital, all
men cannot possess the power to produce the
wealth they need to consume unless a constantly
growing number and proportion of men have
access to the ownership of capital.

Such access to the ownership of capital cannot
be brought about by taking from some who have
too much and giving to others who have too little
or none, for this would be an attempt to maintain

the integrity of private property in capital by means which would destroy it. But it would seem worth considering whether a system of financing new capital formation can be devised which would simultaneously promote the growth of new capital formation and increase the number of households owning viable capital estates.

The alternative, of course, is the alternative which the United States and other countries of the Western world are using: the welfare state's policy of full employment. This is a policy of contriving toil for the sake of making men appear to be productive. It is not questioned by the worker, for he has learned by bitter experience and from history that under the conventional financing system, the ownership of capital is not for him. Nor is it questioned by those who, by accident or inheritance or in some other way, own capital and therefore have access to increasing quantities of newly formed capital. They are not prone to reflect upon the system of conventional finance which frequently gives them access to newly formed capital without regard to their qualifications in other respects.

We have elsewhere stated the underlying principle which we think is applicable here:

> Every man has a natural right to life, in consequence whereof he has the right to maintain and preserve his life by all rightful means, including

the right to obtain his subsistence by producing wealth or by participating in the production of it.[11]

When the great bulk of the wealth is produced by capital instruments, the principle of participation [set forth in the paragraph just quoted] requires that a large number of households participate in production through the ownership of such instruments.[12]

There would seem to be little doubt that conventional business-financing methods fall far short of satisfying this basic principle of economic justice in the United States and in other countries of the Western world today. Nor is the shortcoming through which the non-owner of capital is denied access to capital compensated for by redistributing the wealth produced by capital through artificially contrived toil or artificially priced toil.

C. INFLATION

Inflation is a natural and necessary process in an economy that is capitalistic in its mode of production and laboristic in its form of distribution. Over 70 percent of the wealth produced is distributed to labor, but over 90 percent of that

[11] *The Capitalist Manifesto*, p. 68. See also pp. 77-82.
[12] *Ibid.*, p. 81

wealth is produced, not by labor, but by capital instruments. Quite apart from the manifest injustice
of this imbalance, it is in this ulcerous gap that the
spiral of inflation breeds.[13]

If this analysis is correct, and we think that it
is, then conventional corporate finance, which
brings on this maldistribution of participation in
production through its tendency to concentrate the
ownership of capital, is itself the main and necessary cause of continuous inflation.

At first glance, it might appear that in any
event inflation would tend to counteract the effects
of the growing concentration in the ownership of
capital. Property-less (*i.e.,* capital-less) workers
who borrow money to finance consumption can in
any event pay back their loans in inflation-de-
bauched dollars, thus offsetting the effects of concentration of ownership of capital. However, the
reverse is true.

Consumer credit, which is generally the only
form of credit that is resorted to outside the field of
business finance, bears rates of interest that are
well in excess of any inflation we have suffered so
far. Instead, it is the small savers, the owners of
savings accounts, savings-type insurance policies,
or government bonds, who collectively are the
creditors, that mainly suffer from inflation. A

[13] *Ibid.,* p. 129. See also pp. 130 ff.

corporation that borrows 50 million dollars from one or more insurance companies on a 25-year loan during a period when the annual rate of decline in the purchasing power of the dollar is 2 percent will ultimately have almost half of its loan repaid through inflation. Stated in another way, the small savers whose insurance policies are about as close to capital ownership as they can come—and this is anything but close—will lose about half the purchasing power of their savings to the borrowing corporation over the term of the loan.

Other examples could be given, but the point is clear. Not only does conventional finance make inflation inevitable, but its worst consequence— the intolerable concentration of the ownership of capital—is further intensified by inflation itself.

D. LOSS OF INCENTIVE

In economic matters, an incentive is a reward for production. Our traditional system of corporation finance, however, forces us to penalize rather than reward production.

The owners of capital, who constitute not more than 5 percent of the households of the economy, through the employment of the capital they own, produce the bulk of the wealth. The government is compelled to invade their ownership to redistribute their wealth over the remainder of the population in order to maintain mass consumption. Ownership in the more productive factor of production is rifled to provide adequate incomes for the great number of those who own only the less productive factor.

The disincentive effect of this penalty would undoubtedly be more severe if the owners of capital understood the whole process. Nevertheless, it seems reasonable to assume that an incalculable price is currently being paid in terms of lost production as the result of this inherently disincentive system.

Conversely, it is slowly becoming clear to labor, both organized and unorganized, that the highest wages are not currently being paid for production, but rather for being present at the scene of production as a member of a well-organized power bloc. Indeed, an industrial psychologist of the University of California, in addressing himself to the question "Why are wages paid?" concluded that

> in most cases, what we pay for is attendance, and a minimum of production. Little difference appears in practice in the pay for high production and low production. If a man comes to work on time and stays out of trouble and produces the minimum, he is pretty well assured of his con-

tinued pay. If he produces more, in all likelihood
he is still assured of his continued pay. In general
practice, we do not pay for production, we pay
for attendance.[14]

Conventional finance, through its built-in tendency to foster the massive concentration of the
ownership of capital, is thus both disincentive to
the owners of capital and morally corrosive to
labor. The owners of capital, who produce a
constantly increasing proportion of the total output of wealth, are rewarded by being uncere-
moniously relieved of much of the wealth their
capital currently produces. The owners of labor,
on the other hand, are being taught, by the most
powerful and well-publicized examples, that the
highest rewards are not for production, but for
the employment of organized power to take over a
share of what others produce.

For those who think that we should run an economic race with Russia, where a far lower degree
of industrialization leaves that nation still in a
position of labor shortages which are easily com-
batted with wage incentives, perhaps this doubly
disincentive impediment of our economy is worth
contemplating.

[14] Mason Haire, *Psychology in Management* (1956), p.
126.

E. PRICE DISADVANTAGE
IN INTERNATIONAL TRADE

It is unfortunate that the United States, although employing a system of business finance that is widely imitated by the industrial nations of the free world, has gone much further than these other industrial nations in its system of producing wealth primarily through capital and distributing it principally through labor. This results in labor rates in the United States which are anywhere from two to fifteen times higher than those in competing foreign industrial nations. What this has done, and is going to do, to the foreign trade of the United States—and to its foreign relations if it adopts high tariffs in retaliation—is too well known and understood to require emphasis here.

A happy alternative would be an economy in which the private ownership of capital is so widely diffused that the wealth produced by capital can be distributed to the owners of capital while the economy still maintains a high general standard of living and universal participation in production by all households. In such an economy, prices could fall far below those of the world market, to the great advantage of all concerned. It is clear, however, that no such alternative can come about through our conventional system of financing new capital formation.

F. POLITICAL DISADVANTAGE IN WORLD AFFAIRS

A much longer book would be required fully to catalogue the disadvantages and inadequacies of a system of business finance which ties the ownership of existing capital to the ownership of newly formed capital. We can only call attention to one further serious defect.

There is much evidence that the leaders of many of the underdeveloped economies of the world would like to see their nations industrialized in a manner that would bring about the wide diffusion of privately owned capital. They have no difficulty in seeing that this is a means—very probably the only means—of achieving power diffusion in an industrial society.

The evidence is extensive that the growth of socialism in the underdeveloped countries is encouraged by the inadequacy of the Western system of corporation finance. We will quote one recent commentary:

> In the socialist countries a rapid rate of economic development is made possible by reducing consumption and increasing investment in capital goods. If the underdeveloped nations cannot ob-

tain large amounts of capital by borrowing or by aid they may finally conclude that, to achieve the necessary growth, they must establish a socialist economic system capable of controlling economic resources and diverting them from the production of consumer goods to the production of capital goods . . .

The attitude of the underdeveloped nations toward the competitive struggle for economic power between East and West will not be primarily based on ideology. If they choose a regimented socialist system, they will do so because they are convinced that it is the only way to achieve rapid economic growth . . .

The outcome of the economic struggle for world power will depend not only on the competition between the western and communist powers, but also on the course of development of the underdeveloped nations.

These nations constitute more than two thirds of the world's population. They have vast natural resources and supply a great part of the world's raw materials and food products. Their development will provide expanding markets for manufactured goods. Their share of world trade will grow and their position in the world economy will steadily increase in importance.

Their prospects for success under a system of economic freedom are not very bright. Already many of them are forced to resort to extensive economic controls and restrictions. These may lead to some forms of mixed economy, midway between free enterprise and socialism. The movement of the developing nations away from free enterprise will in itself weaken the economic position of the West.[15]

The conventional method of corporation finance in the free world depends upon the prior accumulation of savings—indeed, great prior accumulations of savings—before it can achieve significant industrial success. The underdeveloped economies neither have accumulations of savings (which would be accumulations of capital) nor do they have the time to wait for such accumulations to come about naturally. They have, one by one, rejected our example for the quicker method of industrialization through socialism. Nor is that all. If they look closely, they can see that constantly to increase the concentration of the ownership of capital is to achieve socialism in the end, but through a slow and painful process. Some of them may even have read the conclusion of one of our foremost economists, that

. . . divorce between men and industrial things is becoming complete. A Communist revolution

[15] "Make Mass Poverty Obsolete," by George Hakim, in *Nation's Business,* May 1960.

could not accomplish that more completely. Certainly it could not do so with the same finesse.[16]

It is clearly in our interest to achieve a private-property, power-diffused economy in the United States. It is equally in our interest to begin spreading capitalism to other nations of the world not only in order that we may realize its ideological power, but also that we may acquire political friends in the world.

It becomes urgent, then, for us to consider whether it is necessary—or indeed in *any* sense desirable—to employ a system of corporation finance, however conventional, that inevitably concentrates the ownership of capital.

G. RESTRICTION OF ECONOMIC GROWTH

If we employ methods of financing new capital formation that use existing capital (*i.e.,* savings) to insure against entrepreneurial error, new capital formation is not merely limited by the amount of existing capital that is not already actively committed to this insurance function, but it is also limited by the extent to which the owners of existing capital or savings will permit their capital or savings to be used for this purpose. In America

[10] Adolf A. Berle, *Power Without Property* (1959), p. 76.

today, the amount of capital or savings available to support new capital formation—particularly the capital held in corporations themselves—is so vast that it does not tend seriously to impede economic growth. The intolerable disadvantage of such a system of finance lies rather in the resulting concentration of the ownership of capital.

This artificial dependence of new capital formation upon the use of existing capital as an insurance fund gets apparent support from a theory still widely held by economists. This is the theory that industrialization is an alternative to high consumption. It is said, for example, that "the richness of America and its ability to set aside without serious inconvenience part of its current production each year for capital accumulation" explains our high rate of capital formation. On the other hand, it is said that "a very poor nation must consume all it produces in order to avoid starvation and to provide the barest minimum of clothing and shelter for its people. Such a nation cannot afford to save; it cannot afford to devote a significant part of its resources to producing capital goods that will raise the productive power and living standard of future generations." [17]

[17] This is taken from a college economics textbook in wide use: *Economics, an Introduction to Analysis and Policy,* by George Leland Bach, Prentice-Hall, 1957, pp. 43-46.

This theory is nonsense when applied—as it generally is—to an economy as a whole. In a study by Harold G. Moulton of The Brookings Institution, made a quarter of a century ago when the funds for capital formation came mostly from market sources, it was clearly demonstrated that new capital formation took place only in response to increases in demand for consumer wealth. Mr. Moulton's analysis left no doubt that high levels of capital formation are reached during periods of high-level consumption.[18] To this we might add the evidence of the second world war, when unprecedented capital formation, unprecedentedly high consumption, and a world's record in *production for destruction* (*i.e.,* non-economic use) were all accomplished simultaneously. *This is something that would be quite impossible if it were physically necessary to have savings precede new capital formation.*

Let us press the examination a step further. Imagine an underdeveloped economy today that is substantially without capital instruments—a pre-industrial economy. Suppose it to possess the natural resources necessary to support industrialization and high-level production. It may have no unemployment, in the sense that every able-bodied individual is engaged in scratching a bare subsistence from the earth, but it has vast amounts of

[18] Harold G. Moulton, *op. cit.,* pp. 157-158.

badly used or underemployed manpower. It has and will have, for the foreseeable future, almost limitless needs, but those who are in need do not have the purchasing power to satisfy their needs. The power to produce wealth is low because the most productive factor of production is missing from the economy. Let us say, further, that while technical know-how is lacking in such a country, it is available for purchase in almost unlimited quantities in other parts of the world—something that was not true when America was in the process of industrializing.

In such an economy, the wealth-producing potential of plants, tools, equipment, railroads, airlines, etc. cannot be questioned from the standpoint of competitive survival. There is no competition. To the extent that the industrialization is carried out through the use of capital instruments whose efficiency has been long demonstrated in other parts of the world, the risk of entrepreneurial error is minimal. All of the necessary physical equipment can be bought in already industrialized nations that are anxious to export it. The period required to build modern industrial plants, or modern railroads, or modern powerhouses, is relatively brief. There are few plants that take more than a year to erect, few hydroelectric installations that cannot be completed in three or four years.

In such an economy, all those who must take

part in the development of industry would inevitably be compensated from the wealth produced by newly formed capital. Some instances of entrepreneurial error would arise. But it would seem that the risk of loss must here be insured by means other than existing savings or capital, for there is none. And it would further seem that traditional finance, looking to already created capital as a fund for the insurance of loss against managerial miscalculation in new capital formation, would greatly impede the rate of new capital formation.

If foreign capital is used here to promote new capital formation in the traditional manner employed by Western economies, the new industries will come into existence under the foreign ownership of those whose capital is used. This, obviously, does not make private enterprise more attractive than socialism to an under-industrialized nation.

Any agency, in short, whether private or governmental, which had the confidence of those whose services and materials are necessary to bring new capital instruments into existence and which obligated itself to channel a portion of the wealth to be produced by the new capital into the reimbursement of those who have participated in its formation, can start the process of industrialization *without resort to past savings*. The agency must be of such stature that its credit is acceptable in trade, or it must have access to bank credit. Nor does it strain the imagination to assume that a method of mutual insurance of the risk of entrepreneurial error can be devised by such an agency, again without resort to past savings.

In a socialist economy, the state is indeed such an agency. This is precisely the reason why the underdeveloped economies of the world are increasingly turning to socialism; for the political pressure on their leaders to bring about industrialization does not leave them time to use the halting methods of traditional finance to induce new capital formation. But in the socialist state, political power is united with economic power through the state's ownership of the most productive factor of production. The inadequacies of Western corporation finance are eliminated, but so is the pattern of power diffusion which is the basis of democratic freedom. Industrialization is achieved at the cost of totalitarianism.

5 *Capital Financing Without Resort to Savings*

Our analysis so far leaves no room for doubt that the traditional financing methods of the West are by no means the only ones possible in an economy in which capital is privately owned. Business has developed many methods for spreading the incidence of losses over large numbers of persons through insurance, in order that individual losses can be held to easily bearable proportions. It is singular, then, that we have not to any significant degree employed an insurance system *as such* in dealing with the risk of entrepreneurial error.

In fact, this failure is no less than remarkable when we have before us the comparable experience of Federal Housing Authority insurance in the field of consumer-goods financing. This insurance protects a lending bank that extends credit to a home buyer. Such a purchaser is generally *not personally liable* on home-purchase money mortgage notes. A failure to pay such a purchase money mortgage note enables the creditor to resort only to the buyer's equity in the residence, but not to obtain a personal judgment against the defaulter. Consequently, there exists for the lender a risk that a home buyer may default on the purchase price and that the market value of the mortgaged house may be less than the balance due on the note at the time of default. FHA insurance covers this risk.

There are no insuperable obstacles to the establishment either through private or governmental means, or through a combination of both, of a system of credit-financing the purchase of newly issued capital stock and of insuring, through either a mutual or funded insurance plan, the risk of entrepreneurial error, which might cause the newly formed capital represented by such stocks to fail to produce sufficient wealth to defray the buyer's cost of acquiring them. We have called attention to this in *The Capitalist Manifesto,* where we suggested that an FHA-type corporation to provide such insurance might be called the Capital Diffusion Insurance Corporation (CDIC).[19] Conventional financing methods, now and heretofore used, restrict new capital formation to those who, through their ownership of savings or existing capital, are in a position to self-insure against the entrepreneurial risks of new capital formation. The proposed CDIC system would simply substitute for the existing self-insurance method a system of mutual or funded insurance to protect banks which finance capital acquisition loans against an excessive coincidence of entrepreneurial errors affecting a financed portfolio of stocks. The essential difference between these alternative systems of financing new capital formation is that the traditional system limits the acquisition of newly formed capital to the owners of existing capital, whereas the CDIC method eliminates savings or the ownership of existing capital as an indispensable factor. [20]

[19] See *The Capitalist Manifesto,* p. 241.

[20] Credit policy considerations might, of course, require a small down payment on the purchase of a financed portfolio, thus still employing savings to this limited extent.

A. FINANCED-CAPITALIST PLAN

We will outline the possible features of a method of simultaneously financing new capital formation and—at the same time—increasing the proportion of households owning viable capital estates (*i.e.,* capital estates of sufficient magnitude that when their financing costs are paid off, they can support, or materially contribute to the support of, a household enjoying a reasonable standard of living). We are fully aware that many, if not all aspects of the plan may be refined and improved.

In general, no new institutions other than the insuring agency itself would be involved, and this would in many ways be similar to the FHA insurance system.

In all probability, the most satisfactory agency for preforming the insurance function would be a public corporation, established and financed initially by Congressional appropriation or by the sale of stock or bonds to the public, and thereafter deriving its income and reserves through fees collected on a proportionate basis from borrowers. The fund would thus provide mutual insurance against the risk that newly formed capital may not produce the wealth expected of it within the predetermined loan period used for financing the purchase of securities representing it.

Already existing financial institutions would make CDIC-insured loans only to *individuals* seeking to acquire equity securities.[21] These would include commercial banks where general industrial trade or professional-service businesses are being established and farm credit banks where agricultural borrowers are involved. Each loan would be made in accordance with policies established by Congress and administered by the Federal Reserve System or by the Capital Diffusion Insurance Corporation, as Congress might determine. The possible contents of these controlling policies we will

[21] Although Harold G. Moulton in 1935 pointed out that increased capital formation could come about in spite of a decline in savings through the use of commercial bank credit, his study was not concerned with the diffusion of capital ownership. See Note 8 above. In principle, the financed-capital plan is not unlike a recent suggestion by the Senate Select Committee on Small Business. The Committee proposed that the Small Business Administration be authorized to insure lease bonds (written by private surety companies) for small retailers, to qualify them to rent space in shopping centers. At the present time, developers cannot finance new shopping-center developments without first leasing most of the space to triple-A tenants (those with net worth of 1 million dollars or more). See the 11th Annual Report, Senate Select Committee on Small Business, January 1960, p. 47

mention later. Such CDIC-insured loans would be made *only* to finance the purchase of newly issued corporate equities, never to finance purchases of outstanding stocks in the secondary market. Since the very function of such a system is to bring into existence a growing number of individual owners of viable capital estates, CDIC loans should not be available to facilitate the purchase of stocks either by corporations or by financial inter-mediaries of any kind.

Maximum limits upon such loans would be necessary, but these would be subject to uniform change from time to time as the conditions of the economy might require. The entire portfolio of securities purchased pursuant to such loans should be pledged to the lending bank to secure the re-payment of the purchase price of the capital estate and payments of interest and insurance on the loan. It would seem desirable, however, under certain conditions, for only part of the income to be withheld for application on the loan obligation of the purchaser of securities. The portion of portfolio income applied through the escrow to payment of the purchase price of the shares in the portfolio might vary with the extent to which the loan has been repaid, or with the extent to which the portfolio has yielded more than the expected return at the time of the loan.

Loans could be, and probably should be, nonrecourse loans, that is, they should not involve the personal liability of the borrower. *The assumption of the risk of failure of the newly formed capital, represented by the various securities in the portfolio, to produce the wealth expected of it at the time the financed-capitalist loan is made, would be the function of the insuring agency, CDIC.* To use personal liability loans for this purpose would be to employ the self-insurance feature which has been responsible for the failure of the existing financing system to promote capital diffusion.

The loan paper received by banks which made CDIC-insured loans to financed capitalists would be made rediscountable by the Federal Reserve Banks, and legislative authority would be granted to Federal Reserve Banks, under proper controls, for the issuance of Federal Reserve Notes against the discounted capital-acquisition loan paper. This system is illustrated by Chart 1, page 64.

Similar arrangements, within the Federal Farm Credit System, could be made for financed-capitalist loans to primarily rural borrowers. It would seem that the same policies should prevail, including the requirement of proper diversification of portfolios.

In *The Capitalist Manifesto,* it was pointed out that both the political and economic essence of private property in productive capital is the right

CHART 1

FINANCING ARRANGEMENTS
OF THE FINANCED-CAPITALIST PLAN

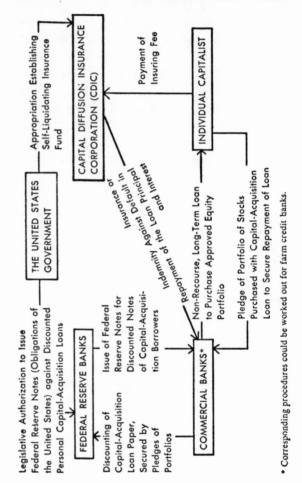

* Corresponding procedures could be worked out for farm credit banks.

CHART 2

HOW CAPITAL INSTRUMENTS PAY
FOR THEMSELVES UNDER
THE FINANCED-CAPITALIST PLAN

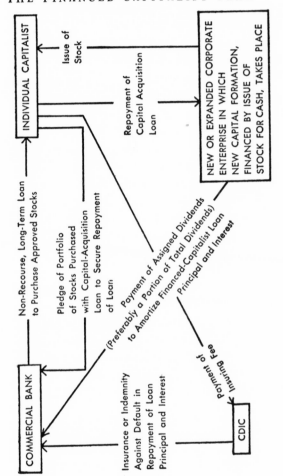

to receive all the wealth produced by that capital. This is impossible unless mature corporations, after setting aside only necessary operating reserves (not reserves for expansion of any kind) pay out 100 percent of their net income to the stockholders.[22] By a "mature corporation" we mean a corporation that has effective access to market sources of capital funds for new capital formation, including funds available for new capital formation through the financed-capitalist program. Thus corporations as a whole would compete in the market for new capital, and the judgments concerning where, when, and how much of the wealth produced by capital to invest and how much to spend on consumption would be left to the property owner—the investor.

The arrangements under which newly formed capital would pay the costs of the new owners in acquiring their portfolios of securities, and would thereafter enable such owners to participate in the production of wealth through capital ownership, is illustrated by Chart 2, page 65.

When capital-acquisition loans have been paid off in full, including principal, interest and insurance fees, the equity portfolio pledged to

[22] See *op. cit.*, Chapter 5 and pp. 210-214. The necessity for tax reforms leading to the eventual repeal of the corporate income tax and the scaling down of personal income taxes is discussed on pp. 169 and 208.

secure the loan would be released to its owner. During the loan period, a substantial opportunity would be afforded the new capitalist, through his contact with the lending bank and its loan advisers, to obtain the elements of an "investor education."

Such questions as how many such loans may be made to a particular household or a particular borrower, the size of capital estate that one could hold before the financed-capitalist facilities would no longer be available, etc., are questions of policy. The correct answers to these questions depend on the rate of technological change, the rate at which households must be withdrawn from the labor market and enter production through capital ownership in order not to have excessive unemployment of non-owners of viable capital estates, and on many other circumstances which we need not state in detail here.

B. CAPITAL DIFFUSION INSURANCE

It is important here to understand the nature of our proposal of capital diffusion insurance. *It does not insure management or shareholders against the risks of business failure.* It only insures a commercial bank, which lends funds to a qualified investor to buy a portfolio of newly issued

stocks, against the risk that the yield on the portfolio will not, within the loan term, defray its
costs of acquisition. Since the entire portfolio
acquired through one or more financed-capitalist
loans would be held in escrow until the purchase
loan had been paid off, the CDIC insurance
would actually provide only ultimate protection
against a *concurrence* of entrepreneurial error in
several of the corporations whose stocks are represented in a well-diversified portfolio.

So far as the financed capitalist is concerned,
shares of stocks that become worthless continue
to be *his* worthless shares. The management of a
business which has issued stock for the purchase
of which CDIC-insured loans have been made
is even more directly affected by the risk of failure.
If the dividends are insufficient, during the financing period, to pay off the financed-capitalist loans
on the corporation's stock, such management must
correct its mistakes and convince "the public"
that its errors have been corrected, or it will not
fare well thereafter in the competitive market for
funds to continue growth. Today, earnings in successful years can be arbitrarily diverted from the
shareholder to offset mistakes that have caused
unsuccessful years.

C. FINANCED-CAPITALIST PLAN AND POWER DIFFUSION FOR A FREE SOCIETY

There is no doubt that government, in the administration of the financed-capitalist program, would exercise considerable power. Is such power reconcilable with the contention that a capitalist economy joined with a political democracy is the ideal power-diffused society? We believe that it is.[23]

In exercising policy-making power through the financed-capitalist program, government employs

[23] The nature of political power is such that it must, particularly in a modern mass-production and mass-communication state, be reasonably centralized to be efficient and effective. American political history has been characterized by legislative, judicial and administrative changes required to increase its efficiency in the face of its large-scale tasks by eliminating much of its original decentralization. Such centralization of political power, however, rather than being offset through the diffusion of economic power in accordance with capitalist principles, has in fact been aggravated by the concentration of economic power in large corporations and in their relatively small group of stockholders and the relentless transfer of economic power to government through the weakening of the private property of individuals in the assets of the great corporations.

only political power. The economic power created through the simultaneous promotion of capital formation and the diffusion of private ownership of capital is privately held and individually exercised economic power—all of it. Through this program, only privately owned capital is created. The power of government is limited to umpiring the rules of the economy, without becoming one of the players.

The protection of private property, without any kind of discrimination, is the first economic rule of a capitalist society. The prime corollary of this first economic rule is the principle that government should never engage in production, nor in the distribution or redistribution of wealth, except such distribution as is involved in protecting the owner of capital or the owner of labor power in the wealth his capital or labor produces.

Under the financed-capitalist plan, the exercise of political power, under constitutional requirements of uniform laws, is accompanied by the creation of private economic power in the form of new capital-owning households, or households in which private ownership of capital is increased and strengthened. The power of government is neither total (*i.e.,* it does not include both political and economic power) nor is there any tendency for it to become total.

It will be seen at once that many policies already long recognized as indispensable to a free-enterprise economy (for example, our anti-trust or anti-monopoly policies) can be made much more effective under the financed-capitalist program than under our present mixed economy.[24]

[24] We do not here suggest that the CDIC system of capital formation should eliminate savings altogether as a means of insuring the risk of entrepreneurial error, but only that an alternative means should be concurrently available which is free of the inherent tendency toward concentration of ownership of capital found in the prevailing system of business and corporate finance. As we suggest in *The Capitalist Manifesto,* such an arrangement, to be effective, might have to be combined with investment preferences for new financed-capitalist estates. See pp. 218-220.

6 *Policy Considerations in Granting Loans under the Financed-Capitalist Plan*

Under the financed-capitalist plan, let us imagine an investment banker counseling his client (an entrepreneur who wishes to launch a new enterprise or to increase the capital facilities of an existing one) to qualify the securities of a corporation so that they would be eligible for financed-capitalist loans to prospective buyers of the stock to be issued. One of the investment banker's principal tasks would be to bring the new issue of securities and the issuing corporation into conformity with the policy requirements laid down by the Federal Reserve Board, the Capital Diffusion Insurance Corporation, or such other body as Congress might designate to interpret its general statutory policies.

Similarly, a prospective purchaser of a portfolio of equity stocks, or of additional stock for an existing portfolio, might go to his bank to arrange a CDIC-insured capital-acquisition loan. In determining the size of the loan for which the prospective borrower is eligible, the commercial banker would be expected to apply the uniform governmental policies established for such loans. Otherwise the loan would not be eligible for rediscount, and the lending power of the bank under the financed-capitalist program would be, to that extent, limited.

What are some of the policy considerations which might be incorporated into the financed-capitalist program?

A. ANTI-MONOPOLY POLICY

Anti-monopoly policy in the United States, Canada, Great Britain and other countries of the free world has been traditionally and, we think, necessarily ineffective. Why? Primarily because it is possible for a corporation which has already grown to such size that the markets in which it buys or sells are no longer freely competitive markets to continue to acquire funds for further growth and intensification of its monopolistic position. In fact, as we have seen, under the ineffective anti-monopoly legislation of these mixed-economy countries, such monopolistic corporations are uniquely able to obtain capital for further expansion and further destruction of competition. When the financed-capitalist program has been established sufficiently long in any economy so that it is the primary source of new capital formation, it will be a relatively simple matter for governmental anti-monopoly policy to be made effective and to keep markets freely competitive. This can be done under uniform policies applicable alike to all similarly situated corporations through control of the capital that can be invested in a corporation which threatens free competition.[25] The benefits attendant upon this aspect of the financed-capitalist program alone would be enormous, for there is no way to calculate the amount of technological advance that is stifled, and the

[25] Under the proposals for legislation we have made to bring about the restoration of private property of corporate stockholders (see *The Capitalist Manifesto,* pp. 207-217), anti-trust control in the maintenance of competitive markets could be exercised through control of the inflow of capital from sources other than financed-capitalist loans, since internal generation of new capital formation by corporations would be prevented.

benefits of lower consumer prices through effective competition that are thwarted, by the present ineffective antimonopoly policies. This financing technique would be a double-edged weapon, diminishing or preventing the flow of capital into corporations which threaten free competition, and encouraging other corporations to enter markets suffering from price administration attendant upon lack of competition.

B. PROMOTION OF TECHNOLOGICAL IMPROVEMENT

One of the goals of a capitalist economy is the production of a maximum amount of wealth with a minimum input of toil. The promotion of technological advance should be a main policy consideration of the financed-capitalist program. Under such a policy, every encouragement would be given to the financing of new enterprises which are being formed or existing enterprises which are being expanded to exploit promising new technical improvements. However, this policy should be tempered by the imposition of high standards for demonstrating feasibility of new enterprises or new expansions before their securities could qualify for CDIC-insured loans.

C. INCREASE IN CAPITAL-OWNING HOUSEHOLDS

The theory of capitalism is inconsistent with the socialist philosophy of the necessity or desirability of full employment, *i.e.,* the employment in the production of wealth of all employables, or all those who would seek employment, without regard to whether there is an economic demand for the increased product. It likewise is inconsistent with the idea that a share of wealth should be distributed as a reward for toil, regardless of whether such toil produces wealth or not. A capitalist economy encourages technological advance as the means by which the burden of the production of wealth may be shifted from labor to capital, thus freeing progressively more men to engage in the work of civilization, and providing them with subsistence to enable them to do so.

To carry out this objective, two things are required. The first is the means of enabling a constantly increasing number of households to participate in the production of wealth through their ownership of capital, and the second is the diminishing of the labor market, *i.e.,* the number of *persons* seeking employment in the production of wealth, so that the value of labor can again be competitively determined without driving wages down to a bare subsistence level.[26]

In brief, a capitalist economy should not seek to contrive toil in order to maintain full employment in the production of wealth. Rather, its task is that of shifting such unemployment to those who can afford it, namely, those who own substantial capital estates.

D. PREVENTION OF CONCENTRATION IN CAPITAL-ACQUISITION

Among policies which might contribute to these objectives in the financed-capitalist program would be policies designed to make the machinery of the program unavailable to those with capital estates that are already monopolistic in size. If this precaution were not taken, the financial institutions of the state would be used, as they are under our mixed economy, to concentrate further the ownership of capital. This in turn would make it necessary, as under our mixed economy, to invade concentrated ownership in order to redistribute income, thus socializing the ownership of capital and substituting the principles of charity or expediency (however disguised) for those of justice in the distribution of wealth. Since the ownership

[26] See *The Capitalist Manifesto*, pp. 220-223.

of capital can be concentrated, while that of labor cannot, the owner of an excessively large capital estate is in the position where he and others similarly situated may so monopolize the production of wealth that they necessarily deprive some households of the opportunity to participate in the production of wealth at all, or to a sufficient extent.

E. INVESTMENT PREFERENCES FOR NEW CAPITALIST ESTATES

We have pointed out elsewhere that the encouragement of the growth in the number of new viable capital estates may well require the adoption of legislation establishing a system of investment preferences, giving new or small capital owners prior access to safer types of stocks.[27] This would leave higher-risk equities to those who are investing savings and who are, generally speaking, in a better position to take higher risks for higher gains. It would be the exact opposite of present practice under which the most promising investments are usually available only to those with the largest capital estates.

[27] *Ibid.*, pp. 218-220.

F. PREVENTION OR DISCOURAGEMENT OF SPECULATION IN STOCKS

Every precaution should be taken to prevent the use of the financed-capitalist program by speculators in securities or for speculative purposes. The financed-capitalist program would make possible the elimination or correction of defects in the American economy—and in other economies of the West—which discourage the acquisition of capital interests *as a means of participating in the production of wealth* and at the same time encourage speculation in capital equities.

Among these existing defects is the steeply progressive personal income tax, particularly when combined with a lower-rate capital gains tax. This ill-conceived combination makes it wiser for the stock buyer to permit corporations to "plow in" earnings to encourage capital gains, rather than to hold his stock for the wealth produced by his invested capital. Such wealth or income, if received as dividends would meet the generally steeper rates of personal income taxes. In those countries which have no capital gains tax at all, the tendency to promote gambling in stocks is, of course, much more pronounced. The simple wisdom of handling one's own capital interests in such manner as to minimize tax confiscation obscures the fact that we are legitimating gambling in equity stocks and discouraging the ownership of capital for the wealth it produces, by all except tax-free financial intermediaries such as charitable trusts.

This deliberate legislative promotion of speculation in stocks to convert some portion of the wealth produced by capital into a gambling profit, taxed as a capital gain or not taxed at all, also obscures the difference between the wealth produced by capital represented by equity stocks and the mere manipulation of stocks to achieve a financial gain entirely independently of the production of wealth at all.

G. CO-ORDINATION OF CONSUMER DEMAND AND NEW CAPITAL FORMATION

In a study which Harold G. Moulton of The Brookings Institute made a quarter of a century ago, it was incontrovertibly demonstrated that in an era when the funds for capital formation came mostly from market sources, new capital formation took place only in response to increases

in demand for consumer wealth.[28] In the inter-
vening twenty-five years, we have slowly changed
our methods of capital formation until today almost three-fourths of new capital formation is
achieved through the internally generated funds of
business enterprises. These funds come primarily
from depreciation, amortization, withheld earnings and depletion allowances under corporate
and personal income tax laws. So distorted has
our economy become under the policies of full
employment, confused tax legislation, laboristic
distribution, and attenuation of the rights of
stockholders that it is not uncommon today to
have capital formation take place far in excess
of the prospective demand for consumer goods to
be produced with the expanded capacity in the
reasonably foreseeable future. Under the financed-
capitalist program, internally generated funds
for new capital formation (as distinguished from
replacement of worn-out capital instruments)
would gradually be eliminated, and in their place

[28] The study also demonstrated something well known to
everyone except the experts: that high levels of capital
formation are reached during periods of high-level consumption. Financial experts are fond of repeating that
increased capital formation is at the expense of immediate consumption, although it ultimately brings
about increased output of consumer goods. *Op. cit.*, pp.
157-158.

would be the equity investments of individuals, financed either through capital-acquisition loans or through the investment of savings. One of the policy considerations affecting the volume of CDIC-insured loans would be the need for keeping the capital wealth-producing capacity in line with the aggregate desire of the economy for consumer goods and with the actual defense needs of the nation—as distinguished from full-employment schemes made more palatable under the disguise of defense needs.

H. INFLATION CONTROL
AND CONCURRENT REDUCTION
OF CONSUMER CREDIT

Money and credit, being merely representative of real wealth, cannot expand at a faster rate than real wealth without bringing about inflation. A just economy requires a stable currency of uniform purchasing power. Consequently, it would be both necessary and desirable, in order to avoid an inflationary effect through the accumulation of purchasing power in excess of available production, that the expansion of credit in the financing of capital formation be accompanied by a contraction of credit in the consumer field. Such a program would also tend toward the ultimate objective of a capitalist economy in which the dominant source of purchasing power is the income directly derived from capital ownership and labor ownership by the individual participants in production and in which consumer credit plays a diminished part.

This is but another aspect of the tendency of a capitalist economy to equalize *participation in production,* as distinguished from the tendency of a socialist economy or our mixed economy merely to equalize consumption irrespective of contribution to production.

The inflationary danger of massive purchasing power accumulated in the highly concentrated estates of the largest capitalist households and in the semi-socialized trusts or foundations to which these estates are customarily transferred today under the threat of tax confiscation would be eliminated as these estates were diffused, through normal transfers by gifts and bequests, under legislative changes designed to encourage transfers to submonopolistic beneficiaries.[29]

I. ENCOURAGEMENT OF EQUITY FINANCING AND DISCOURAGEMENT OF DEBT FINANCING

The economic and political objectives of a capitalist society can be achieved only through widely

[29] See *The Capitalist Manifesto,* pp. 192-199.

diffused private ownership of productive capital. This is to say that direct common-stock ownership is, from the capitalist point of view, a preferable method of financing capital formation, and that debt financing, other than the use of credit to finance acquisition of equity portfolios by individuals, should eventually be extinguished. Debt financing by corporations is a device for weakening the property of the owner of small "savings" in his capital because both the benefits and control of such capital interests generally fall into the hands of financial intermediaries. Furthermore, debt financing facilitates the concentration of ownership of the already great capital estates, while separating the owner of savings from the responsibilities and advantages of capital ownership. Unquestionably, one of the policy considerations which would dominate the financed-capitalist plan would be the promotion of equity ownership, the discouraging of direct debt financing of capital formation, and the elimination of types of financial intermediaries that impair or frustrate a healthy, direct equity ownership of industry by a growing proportion of the individuals of the economy.

On its face a proposal to gradually substitute common-stock financing for debt financing in capital formation would appear to be a change of considerable magnitude, but actually the change is more apparent than real. In bulk, the protective provisions of loan agreements, mortgages and the like are aimed at shielding creditors against large-scale default by borrowers in the event of a major depression. However, it is reasonably certain that any major depression of the future will be looked upon, legislatively and politically, as a man-made catastrophe, and that any wholesale enforcement of debt obligations would be prohibited. Thus in reality capital formation on the whole is, from the risk standpoint, though not in economic effect, equity financing whether it is called such or not. The truth of this statement is further evidenced by the fact that today even the occasional defaults that arise under loan agreements and mortgages generally result only in an administrative compromise, with the creditor assisting the debtor in the working out of a difficult position. It would therefore appear that in the majority of cases capital funds obtained under loan agreements are in substance treated as equity investments.

J. PERSONAL APTITUDES AND EDUCATIONAL REQUIREMENTS

Many of the most important and difficult policies in the administration of the financed-capitalist program would be those formulated by Congress and by the agencies designated by Congress to determine the eligibility requirements of individuals for CDIC-insured capital-acquisition loans.

The difficulties in establishing such policies are those of human adaptability. Throughout the period of man's existence on earth, he has never before been able to produce a comfortable supply of economic goods and services for large numbers of people, while employing for this purpose but a fraction of human capacity for toil. Can human beings survive substantial freedom from subsistence toil?

It is clear that in the past limited numbers of people, wholly freed from the necessity of personal labor to satisfy their economic wants, have used the leisure thus afforded them to devote their creative energies to the arts, sciences, literature, statesmanship, invention, religion, education, discovery—in short, to the works of civilization. Most of our cultural and scientific heritage is the product of such men of leisure.

But examples to the contrary abound. Many men, freed from the energy-sapping, time-consuming requirements of personal labor for subsistence, and being furnished with a comfortable and secure supply of goods and services, have permitted themselves to fall into idleness, lasciviousness, perpetual play, or other mischief. Still others, apparently failing to distinguish between the means to a good life and the living of a good life once adequate means are assured, continue feverishly to produce and accumulate more of the means— *i.e.,* more wealth.

A capitalist society would cast out the irrational doctrine of full employment. As more and more of its wealth is produced by capital and less by labor, more households would participate in the production of wealth as owners of capital and fewer as owners of labor. The number of persons in the "labor market," *i.e.,* seeking paid employment in producing wealth, would progressively be reduced by tax legislation designed to keep owners of large capital estates from taking employment opportunities from households whose only means of participating in production is through their labor.[30] As a result, enlightened men and women owning viable capital estates would come to see that the world is full of many things more attractive than excessive wealth-getting and many creative activities more inherently satisfying than toil for subsistence.

But would the majority of owners of substantial capital estates, thus released from toil for subsistence, follow the pattern of the virtuous men of leisure?

[30] *Ibid.,* pp. 220-223.

One of the reasons why this question is so difficult to answer is that up to the present *we have continued to delude ourselves that the purpose of technological advance is to provide full employment*. So long as we cling to this nonsense, it seems futile to begin educating children and adults alike to comprehend the limited (if still considerable) extent to which human toil is either necessary or capable of producing wealth in an industrialized society. Yet the glaring lesson of technology is clear for all to see: while the toil requirements for producing subsistence are limited, the leisure-work requirements of civilization are unlimited.

Thus the question comes down to whether men and women, who in general recognize that *they must work in order to be happy,* are so short-sighted that they can see and understand only the more animal forms of work—work to produce wealth—or whether they can come to see that the most important, most productive, and least explored tasks of mankind on earth lie above and beyond the subsistence field. The question is perplexing beyond measure, for *it is a question that could never have been asked before.*

There is no doubt as to how socialism deals with this question. Karl Marx propounded the false labor theory of value. This is the theory that only labor produces wealth, regardless of how much capital and how few workers may actually be employed in any process of production. All socialists, from Marx on down, worship subsistence toil.

On September 21, 1958, Nikita S. Khrushchev published a long discourse on Soviet education, condemning the graduates of Russian high schools and colleges for being "unfit" for anything except higher study, even though the higher institutions of learning did not "need" additional teachers. Furthermore, he charged, these graduates have come to regard heavy toil as the proper lot of those who have failed to get higher educations. Khrushchev proposed as a slogan for the new program "that all children must prepare for *useful* labor and participation in the building of Communist society."

It would seem that as the Russian economy approaches a state of industrialization comparable to ours, either its totalitarian masters will be faced with a large-scale revolt of slaves who see the possibilities of freedom in an industrial society, or these rulers will maintain the full employment of everyone but artists and infants in the tasks of producing wealth and war. It is doubtful whether the slave state of socialism can survive in an industrial age without "full employment" and, conversely, whether *full employment* can survive in an advanced industrial society without

bringing about the socialization or collectiviza-
tion of that society.

Among the proper pursuits of the constantly
growing proportion of men in a capitalist society
whose participation in production is largely or
entirely through their ownership of capital is the
defense of their nation. There would seem to be
less danger, however, that this opportunity would
be abused to create an aggressive militarist state
than that the over-building of defense or war
establishments will arise, under a mixed or social
economy, out of the use of military programs to
provide full employment.

This brief discussion of an involved problem
should at least suffice to indicate how important
it will be, in granting capital-acquisition loans to
individual households, to see that eligibility requirements include the possession of sufficient
economic knowledge wisely to husband, manage
and preserve a capital estate, or at least the aptitude and willingness to acquire such knowledge
during the pledge period of the loan. It should
be equally apparent that the educational back-
ground of applicants for capital-acquisition loans
would be an important qualification. Such educational requirements might be met through formal
schooling in schools and colleges, or it might be
met by other means, but they should in any event
provide some basis for hope that the freedom

from personal toil which can be achieved through capital acquisition would be constructively used to contribute to the work of civilization.[31]

We can reasonably expect that the establishing of substantial aptitude and educational requirements for borrowing under the financed-capitalist program should have a quite different effect upon the general level of mental attainments of the people than has the practice of laboristic distribution in our mixed economy. The primary tool of laboristic distribution for maintaining prosperity and full employment is successive and unrelenting injections of great quantities of purchasing power into the economy. While this is achieved by direct government redistribution of income, by subsidizing various high-employment occupations and industries and other well-known techniques, one of its more effective means is the raising of wages far above their competitive value through legalizing and supporting monopoly labor practices and through legislative underpinning of wages.

From the standpoint of education, this has had the effect of subsidizing the refusal of increasing numbers of potential students to enter higher education. We are today bemoaning the inadequacy of the number of candidates for careers as scientists, engineers, lawyers, doctors, teachers

[31] See *The Capitalist Manifesto,* pp. 244-251.

and as members of the other learned professions. With the empty materialism characteristic of the mixed economy, we attempt to offset this entirely normal effect of the synthetic elevation of wages by devising various ways to subsidize higher education. This is another battle of subsidies, comparable to the subsidizing of agricultural prices and the counter-subsidizing of wages to enable workers to pay for higher-priced foods.

The financed-capitalist program would not only gradually eliminate the false values attached to toil, but could also give enormous impetus to the search for self-improvement through education, by imposing gradually rising educational requirements upon applicants for capital-acquisition loans.

7 *The Function of the Investment Banker under the Financed-Capitalist Plan*

We have already noted the importance to the financed-capitalist program of commercial banks and other lending institutions accustomed to making loans to individuals. Since the investment banker is not normally a "banker" at all in the sense of being part of the national monetary and credit system, what could we expect the functions of the investment banker to be under the financed-capitalist program?

Today, investment banks (or investment

houses) are, together with the registered stock exchanges, the main factors in providing the facilities for the trading in outstanding securities. They are, among other things, the principal agencies in what is generally called the "secondary market" to distinguish it from the primary market in which the newly issued securities are placed with investors.

In general, we should expect that, in a financed-capitalist economy, two dominant tendencies would influence the secondary stock market. One would be the suppression of speculation or gambling in stocks, which are representative of the chief means of production in an industrial economy. Speculation in stocks is both tolerated and encouraged today because of the lack of understanding of the nature of a capitalist economy. It is neither more necessary nor more justifiable to encourage speculation in securities representative of the means of production than it would be to gamble with the labor power of workers—the other active factor of production.

The principles of economic justice, which are central to a capitalist economy, assert that wealth should be distributed to those who produce it. *They also imply that the acquisition of wealth, other than through voluntary gifts, or genuine changes in value through changes in supply or demand, by those who contribute nothing to its pro-*

duction, is the height of injustice.[32] The common justification for secondary-market speculation, aside from the necessity for orienting business transactions to ill-conceived tax laws, is that an active secondary market is necessary to "season" the securities of various corporations so that issuers can thereafter more easily obtain new capital when they seek it. This defense of the speculative stock market is almost groundless even in our present mixed economy, since only a minute portion of new capital formation is derived from the issuance of stock to investors in the market. The argument would be totally untenable in a capitalist economy. Under the financed-capitalist program, the ease with which corporations would acquire new capital through the sale of stocks would depend wholly upon the wealth-producing prospects of their capital-expansion proposals, and not upon the behavior of their stocks in a largely irrational speculative market.

Thus we might expect that the de-emphasizing of speculation in stock, and the emphasizing of investment in new capital formation, would bring about a tendency to reduce all forms of activity relating to the secondary market in stocks.

However, the other dominant tendency we have referred to would have an opposite effect. The inducement to finance the acquisition of new

[32] See *The Capitalist Manifesto,* pp. 66-69.

capital estates would far more than offset the tendency to suppress speculation, in terms of the volume of securities handled by investment houses or brokerage houses and stock exchanges. One of the goals of a capitalist economy is the financing of new capital formation entirely through the issuance of equity stocks directly to individual investors. The extent to which this would increase the volume of securities outstanding is incalculably great. Nor can there be any doubt of the desirability of a sound and active secondary market, in which market value would reflect, predominantly if not exclusively, the wealth-producing history and prospects—in the opinion of buyers and sellers—of the capital represented by such stocks.

What of the so-called investment-banker function? This function in the present mixed economy has been aptly described by Professor Merwin H. Waterman as that of a "transporter" of funds from the "savers" to those who would use the funds in capital formation.[33]

While the financed-capitalist program would not exclude the investment of savings in new capital formation, it would provide a limitless alternative source of new capital formation. Furthermore, in the long run, the diffusion of

[33] *Investment Banking Functions* (1958), pp. 2, 11, 16, 20 and 56.

private ownership of capital resulting from the guidance of new capital formation would eliminate the dominant tendency, present in a primitive capitalist economy and in the mixed economy, for savings and capital ownership endlessly to grow and concentrate in a geometric progression. The gigantic accumulations of savings (property rights in which are increasingly attenuated) would tend to fade out, while submonopolistic capital estates would proliferate. Nevertheless, to the extent that savings would be available for investment, the investment banker would continue to be a transporter of funds between the saver and the user of new capital.

Far more important than the mere selling to corporations of their influence with or access to the owners of concentrated savings would be the functioning of the investment banker as the "attending physician" at the birth of new productive capital instruments and of new firms employing them. In this capacity, the investment banker would be charged with qualifying the stocks of new enterprises, or of existing enterprises seeking new capital, for financing through the financed-capitalist program. This function of investment bankers we might call their "entrepreneurial service" function.

Through their entrepreneurial-service function, investment bankers would bring to bear their expertise in the financial field to counsel issuers of stocks how to meet and satisfy the CDIC requirements in order that the stock to be financed would be eligible for financed-capitalist loan insurance. Thus their functions in this capacity would involve the articulation of the work of engineers, accountants, lawyers, marketing experts and all others whose services are required so to plan, design, and establish either a new enterprise or additions to existing enterprises that the newly formed capital will in fact "throw off" or produce the wealth that is expected of it. No service in the economy would be in greater demand or have greater importance than this function of the investment banker. It is at the point of rendering the entrepreneurial advice and counsel of investment bankers to new issuers that the extent of entrepreneurial error and the demands upon the CDIC insurance fund would be minimized.

8 *Financed-Capitalist Plan and Economic Growth*

A. UNDERDEVELOPED ECONOMIES

The socialist theorists make much of what they regard as the questionable efficiency of the present mixed economy to "allocate" resources between current consumption and capital formation in such a way as to promote the growth and best interests of the economy as a whole. They would prefer to see, of course, the totalitarian control that necessarily exists in any socialist economy—for example that of Russia—where the "New Class" of ruling bureaucrats makes this determination. The fact of the matter is that the apparent necessity for "allocation" between present consumption and capital formation, except in those economies that suffer a shortage of labor, raw materials, or technical know-how, is the result of nothing more than an *institutional defect* in the capital-forming process.

The moment that financial savings cease to be the sole source of capital formation, and there is established instead the financed-capitalist program under which capital formation becomes a process of organizing the construction and equipping of plants, buildings, transportation lines, farms, etc., and of channeling a portion of the wealth produced by new capital instruments to pay those who participated in "forming" them (or the reimbursing of credit advanced for this purpose), then the idea of "allocation" is eliminated from the picture.

There is no practical limitation under the financed-capitalist plan on the amount of credit available to finance the purchase of equity stocks in new or expanded enterprises, so long as the physical need exists for the wealth to be produced by newly formed capital. It is the function of governmental and private financing institutions to make certain that participation in production either through capital ownership or through labor ownership, is open to all households of the economy. Such participation in production, either through furnishing labor or through the ownership of productive capital, is the source of purchasing power for use in immediate consumption. Only where a shortage of labor, raw materials, or know-how exists would there be any reason to choose, under the financed-capitalist plan, between increased consumption and new capital formation. In all other instances, new capital formation and personal consumption would normally expand simultaneously.

While this realization is of momentous significance for economies like those of the United States, Canada or Great Britain, *it is of even greater importance to the economies of the underdeveloped countries.* The latter frequently do have an abundance of labor, resources, land, and access in the world market to sufficient know-how, but very little accumulated wealth or savings. Using capitalist principles, particularly the financed-capitalist program, these underdeveloped economies can, either with or without self-liquidating loans from more affluent nations, engage in steady and effective programs of capital expansion and at the same time experience a growth in the number of individual owners of capital who need have no guilt complex that they have been wards of foreign charity. As it is today, the small amount of accumulated wealth in such economies operates as a close limitation upon industrialization, and forces them either to resort to international charity or to become industrialized in a socialist manner.

The recognition that entrepreneurial error can be adequately insured to promote capital formation without resort to accumulated wealth or savings is of the greatest significance to the under-industrialized economies of the world. From the political standpoint, we need have no doubt about the view of communism that will be taken by households which become new owners of viable capital estates in such economies.

The over-all importance, then, of a change from the traditional Western methods of financing capital formation to capital formation dependent increasingly upon the financed-capitalist program rests upon the fact that the extent of accumulated savings need never again constitute a limitation upon capital formation.

B. ELIMINATION OF RESTRICTIONS ON ECONOMIC GROWTH

Another limiting factor in the rate of new capital formation under the traditional private financing methods employed by Western nations is also directly connected with the existing relation be-

tween accumulated savings and new capital formation. This is the reluctance on the part of many
owners of the largest holdings of accumulated
wealth to permit their savings to be used in new
enterprises, or even in any but the safest (and
frequently most monopolistic) of existing enterprises, simply because their incentive to acquire
further wealth is replaced by a supervening interest in protecting what they have, or because
their capacity to supervise their investments cannot be spread any thinner.[34] The financed-capitalist program would eliminate this drawback to new
capital formation. It may be expected that it
would also eliminate much of the frustration which
new entrepreneurs experience today when they
seek funds for their enterprises.

There is one further impediment to capital formation that would be eliminated by the financed-
capitalist plan. Taking their cue from Adam
Smith's observation that "capitals are increased
by parsimony," bankers, economists, and even
businessmen are sometimes heard to say that if
people would spend less (*i.e.,* save part of their

[34] It must be acknowledged that this tendency is some-
what offset by high income taxation against which business losses may be offset. However reluctant taxpayers
may be to risk their own wealth, they sometimes do not
hesitate to take even unreasonable risks with "tax
dollars."

earnings) and invest more, we could have a growing capitalist class. The difficulty with this idea
(part and parcel of the theory that capital formation must be only a "transporting" of existing
wealth or savings) is that the only purpose of capital expansion is *increased* consumption, and it is
increased consumption that is normally and prop-
erly the cause of capital expansion.[35] Unless
capital formation is a response to actual or in-
cipient increase in consumer demand, overproduc-
tion, idle plant capacity and the elements of a
recession are introduced into the economy. Under
the financed-capitalist program, the simultaneous
expansion of capital equipment and of consumption are not only possible but also normal, just as
through the use of credit financing of the war effort
(unfortunately not self-liquidating except in the
non-financial sense) an enormous expansion of
capital outlays, consumption, and war destruction
were simultaneously financed.

The significant thing to be noted here is that in
the American economy, as in the Canadian and
other economies where resources are adequate,
neither land, nor resources, nor technological
know-how have generally been limiting factors to
new capital formation. Rather, the limiting factor

---

[35] This was made clear by Harold G. Moulton, (see *op.
cit.*, particularly pp. 157-158). The lesson seems largely
forgotten.

has been inadequate knowledge of the principles of a capitalist economy, and the consequent failure of financing institutions to perform their proper tasks. New capital formation—economic growth —has been artificially and needlessly limited by the availability of savings or existing capital ownership which could insure against entrepreneurial error in the traditional process of new capital formation. From time to time industry itself, in a narrow sense, has recognized the absurdity of this limitation. For example, Jones and Lamson, a major machine tool builder, argued in a full-page ad that its no-down-payment lease plan would jump over this obstacle and enable manufacturers to acquire 10 billion dollars' worth of new, highly productive machine tools which could be paid for out of increased output.[36]

[36] *Wall Street Journal,* February 4, 1960, p. 10.

9 *Significance of the Financed-Capitalist Plan: Reversing the Trend Toward Socialism and Building a Capitalist Economy*

The practical implications of the discovery that new *personal* capital formation (*i.e.*, newly formed capital that is individually owned) can come into existence independently of financial savings are broader than we can begin to explore in this essay. But the most important of the possibilities envisaged is the vast power of the financed-capitalist plan to build capitalist economies.

It is, for example, immediately apparent that under a financed-capitalist system of economic growth, there is no relationship between the size of an industrial undertaking and the ability of private business to carry it out. Using the capital diffusion insurance method, it is quite as easy to achieve widely diffused private ownership in financing the construction of a multi-billion-dollar project as in the financing of a ten-thousand-dollar project. It would be as feasible to convert the Hoover Dam or the Tennessee Valley Authority into a business privately owned by hundreds of thousands of individual shareholders as it was for the West German Republic recently to convert the Volkswagen Company into a privately owned corporation.

Socialist methods of new capital formation are more efficient and quicker than the traditional methods of business finance now employed by the free world. But the socialist technique places ownership of newly formed capital in the State, and thus is incapable of taking advantage of the powerful latent desire of all men to acquire *as their private property* the ownership of productive capital. It was this desire personally to own productive capital that caused the great industrial advances of the United States, Great Britain, Germany, and the other industrial nations of the free world during the past century. As we have shown, however, the desire to own productive capital has been effectively thwarted for all but a small minority by the traditional methods of corporation finance which limit eligibility to acquire newly formed capital to those who already own capital.

The financed-capitalist plan would end this frustration. It can not only make possible the industrialization of underdeveloped economies in a manner that employs the powerful incentive of private ownership, but it can also bring about the most rapid growth of new capital formation achievable by any means.

Of even greater importance for the American economy is the fact that, through the method of financing new capital formation which we have outlined, the economic race between the free world and the communist world can be placed in its proper perspective, and our chances of winning it can be increased immeasurably. No longer would the issue merely be one of whether socialist methods or traditional Western methods of bringing about economic growth can create the higher standard of living. Rather, the rivalry would be between a totalitarian technique of forcing industrialization by mandate upon a propertyless and freedomless people, and a capitalist system of simultaneously creating a high level of wealth production and consumption along with conditions of maximum individual freedom and maximum personal incentive.   We have no reservations in predicting that, on this basis, the West can win.

LOUIS O. KELSO

Born in Denver, Colorado, in 1913, Louis Kelso was educated in the public and parochial schools of that city and its suburbs. He graduated from the University of Colorado in 1937, where he received his LL.B. in 1938.

Mr. Kelso is a corporate and financial lawyer, economist and lecturer. He heads a major San Francisco law firm, where he has practiced since 1947. From 1938 to 1942 he practiced law in a large firm in Denver, specializing in municipal bond financing and public finance law. He served as a Naval Intelligence officer during World War II and held the position of Associate Professor of Law at the University of Colorado during 1946. He is a member of the board of trustees of the Institute for Philosophical Research in San Francisco.

Mr. Kelso is coauthor with Dr. Adler of *The Capitalist Manifesto,* from which this book is derived.

MORTIMER J. ADLER

Born in New York City in 1902, a graduate of its public schools and of Columbia, where he also received his Ph.D., Mortimer Adler taught at Columbia University from 1923 to 1929, and then at the University of Chicago from 1930 to 1952, where he was for many years Professor of the Philosophy of Law. In 1952 he left Chicago to establish in San Francisco the Institute for Philosophical Research, of which he is now President and Director.

Dr. Adler is one of the original instigators of the great-books program in liberal arts colleges and in adult education. He is a director of the Great Books Foundation, and was Associate Editor of *Great Books of the Western World* and Editor of *The Great Ideas*, a Syntopicon, published by Encyclopaedia Britannica.

Author of the popular best seller, *How to Read a Book*, Dr. Adler has written books about a wide variety of subjects, among them *Art and Prudence*, *What Man Has Made of Man*, *A Dialectic of Morals*, *How to Think about War and Peace*. With Father Walter Farrell, O.P., he published in *The Thomist*, between 1941 and 1944, a series of articles on the Theory of Democracy directly relevant to the thesis of *The Capitalist Manifesto*. He has recently written a two-volume work entitled *The Idea of Freedom*.